Investigations

# Rolling

Patricia Whitehouse

Heinemann Library
Chicago, Illinois

a division of Reed Elsevier Inc.
Chicago, Illinois

Customer Service 888-454-2279
Visit our website at www.heinemannlibrary.com



Designed by Sue Emerson, Heinemann Library; Page layout by Que-Net Media
Printed and bound in the United States by Lake Book Manufacturing, Inc.
Photo research by Beth Chisholm

07 06 05 04 03
10 9 8 7 6 5 4 3 2 1

**Library of Congress Cataloging-in-Publication Data**
Whitehouse, Patricia, 1958-
Rolling / Patricia Whitehouse.
p. cm. – (Investigations)
Includes index.
Summary: Presents simple hands-on experiments that demonstrate the properties that make rolling easier or more difficult.
ISBN: 1-4034-0907-2 (HC), 1-4034-3470-0 (Pbk.)
1. Rolling contact–Juvenile literature. [1. Motion–Experiments. 2. Experiments.] I. Title.
TJ183.5 .W48 2003
530.11–dc21
2002014425

**Acknowledgments**
The author and publishers are grateful to the following for permission to reproduce copyright material:
Cover and interior photographs by Que-Net/Heinemann Library



Special thanks to our advisory panel for their help in the preparation of this book:

Alice Bethke,
Library Consultant
Palo Alto, CA

Kathleen Gilbert,
Second Grade Teacher
Round Rock, TX

Jan Gobeille, Kindergarten Teacher
Garfield Elementary
Oakland, CA

Eileen Day,
Preschool Teacher
Chicago, IL

Sandra Gilbert,
Library Media Specialist
Fiest Elementary School
Houston, TX

Angela Leeper,
Educational Consultant
North Carolina Department
of Public Instruction
Wake Forest, NC

Some words are shown in bold, **like this.**
You can find them in the picture glossary on page 23.

# Contents

# What Is Rolling?

Rolling is a way things move.

Rolling things turn over and over.

Some shapes roll.

Other shapes do not roll.

# Do Round Things Roll?

This ball is on a **smooth** floor.

Gently push the ball.

The ball rolls.

**Round** things will roll easily on something smooth.

Now the ball is on a carpet.

Gently push the ball.

The ball rolls.

But it does not roll as far on the **rough** carpet.

# Can a Tube Roll?

Lay a paper towel **tube** on its side.

Then push the tube.

The tube rolls across the floor.

The side of the tube is **round**.

Stand the **tube** on one end
and push.

The ends of the tube are not **round**.

The tube falls down.

# Can a Pencil Roll?

Lay a pencil on the floor.

**Flick** it with your finger.

The pencil rolls across the floor.

But look closely—it is not **round**.

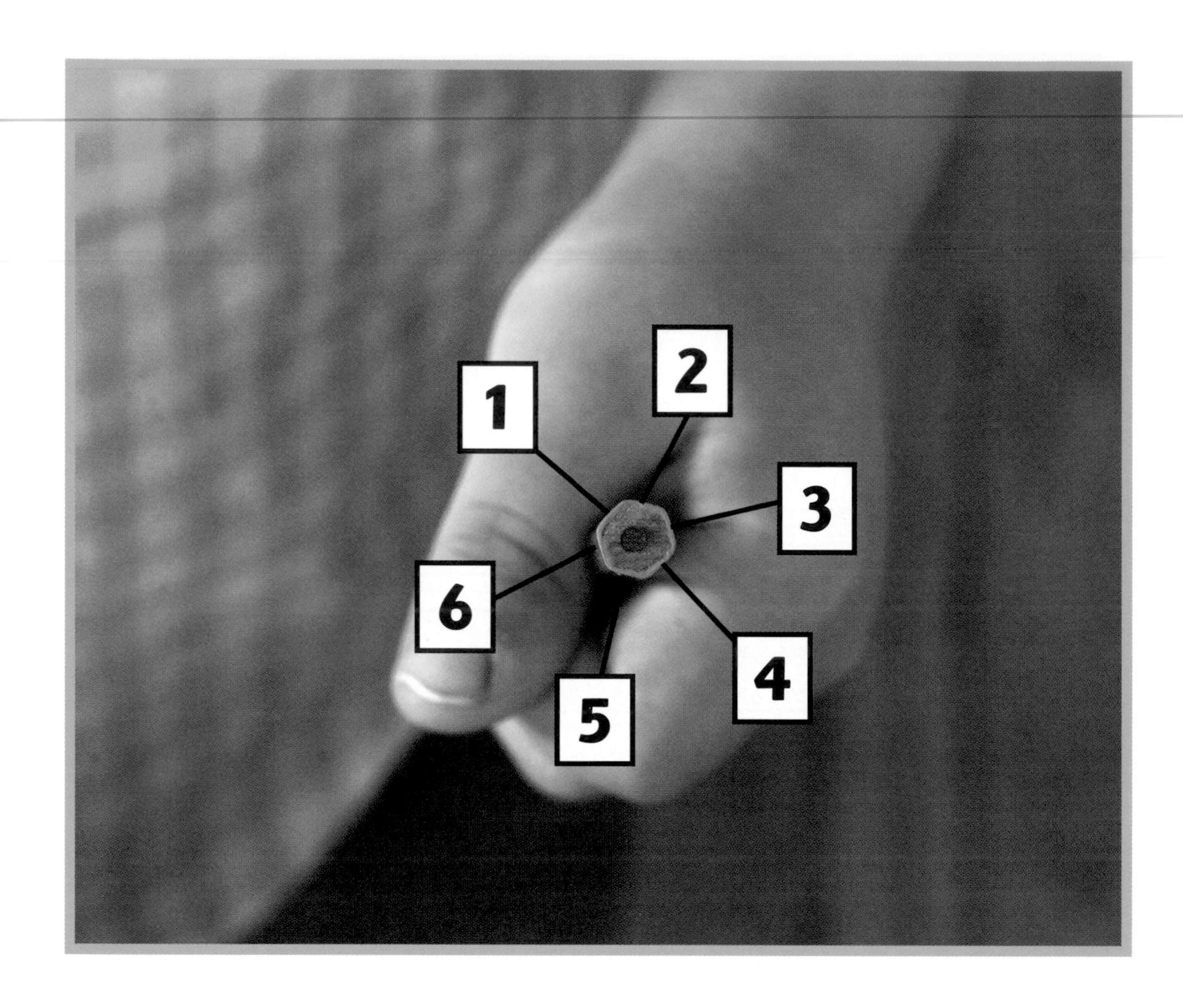


This pencil has six sides.

The six sides give the pencil a **rounded** shape.

Things with a rounded shape roll.

But they need a bigger push.

# Can a Block Roll?

Put a block on the floor.

Then push the block.

The block does not roll.

It does not have a **rounded** shape.

Now push the block harder.

What happens?

The block **tumbles.**

But it does not roll.

# Quiz

Which things can roll?

Look for the answer on page 24.

# Picture Glossary

**flick**
page 14

**rough**
page 9

**round**
pages 7, 11, 12, 15, 16, 17, 18

**smooth**
pages 6, 7

**tube**
pages 10, 11, 12, 13

**tumble**
page 21

# Note to Parents and Teachers

Through play, children examine the physical world and various forces of nature that affect it. This book extends child's play into experiments about the physics of rolling objects. Through these experiments, children explore how the shape of an object affects its ability to roll. The experiments use materials that can be found around the home and classroom, so children can repeat an experiment they read about.

Before reading the book with children, show them objects from the book and ask them which will roll and why they think so. Then, read each chapter, do the experiments, and talk about what you have learned. For example, after reading pages 14 and 15, have the children roll a pencil across the floor. Then read pages 16 and 17, and have the children closely examine the pencil to see its rounded shape. Help children find other objects that have a rounded shape and have them guess whether they will roll.

CAUTION: Children should not attempt any experiment without an adult's permission and help.

# Index



**Answer to quiz on page 22**

The ball, paper towel tube, and pencil can roll.